Developing an E-Health Strategy

A Commonwealth Workbook of Methodologies, Content and Models

Tom Jones

COMMONWEALTH
SECRETARIAT

Commonwealth Secretariat
Marlborough House
Pall Mall
London SW1Y 5HX
United Kingdom

Published by the Commonwealth Secretariat
Edited by editors4change Ltd
Designed by S.J.I. Services, New Delhi
Cover design by Tattersall Hammarling and Silk
Printed by Hobbs the Printers, Totton, Hampshire

Copies of this publication may be obtained from
Publications Section
Commonwealth Secretariat
Marlborough House
Pall Mall
London SW1Y 5HX
United Kingdom
Tel: +44 (0)20 7747 6534
Fax: +44 (0)20 7839 9081
Email: publications@commonwealth.int
Web: www.thecommonwealth.org/publications

A catalogue record for this publication is available from the British Library.

ISBN (paperback): 978-1-84929-032-6
ISBN (e-book): 978-1-84859-083-0

Foreword

It is with great pleasure that I present the 'Developing an E-Health Strategy' workbook. This has been developed in recognition of the immense value that new technologies can bring to health access, the training of health personnel and the strengthening of management information systems.

The Health Section of the Social Transformation Programmes Division at the Commonwealth Secretariat was mandated by Commonwealth Health Ministers in 2008 to assist member countries in strengthening their health systems through the use of information and communication technology (ICT). Since that time, we have undertaken research, policy dialogues, explored public–private partnerships and implemented e-health pilot projects to enhance the use of ICT in the health systems of our member countries.

This workbook addresses requests made by member countries for a practical guide to developing and implementing e-health strategies. The methodologies and models offered within the workbook meet this request, offering examples from countries to enable the sharing of best practice and cover the essential topics of leadership, affordability and a step-by-step guide to policy development.

I am confident that this workbook will prove to be a useful tool in your own country's progression towards developing or strengthening its own e-health strategy. The Commonwealth Secretariat remains committed to promoting e-health not as a standalone programme, but as support to the ongoing efforts within member countries.

Dr Sylvia J Anie (CSci, CChem MRSC)
Director
Social Transformation Programmes Division
Commonwealth Secretariat

Acknowledgements

The Commonwealth Secretariat is grateful for the help and support of many people in government ministries, health services, non-governmental organisations (NGOs) and information and communications technology (ICT) vendors in several countries who contributed to developing the e-health policy and strategy methodology and templates. The methodology and templates reflect their valuable contributions.

To download the methodology and templates, visit the links at the Commonwealth Secretariat's website at: http://www.thecommonwealth.org/ehealth. The file is in Microsoft Word so users can modify the tables to match their specific needs.

Material prepared by *TanJent* Consultancy, UK.

Contents

List of acronyms and abbreviations

AHI	Africa Health Infoway
CAN	Capacity, applications and reliable networks
CPOE	computerised physician order entry
ECSA	East, Central and Southern African Health Community
EHR	electronic health records
EPR	electronic patient records
EU	European Union
FBO	faith-based organisation
GDP	gross domestic product
ICD	WHO's International Statistical Classification of Diseases
ICT	information and communications technology
MDGs	Millennium Development Goals
MP	mobile phones
NGO	non-governmental organisation
PACS	picture archiving and communications systems
PPP	public–private partnership
PCAN	portable capacity, applications and reliable networks
WHO	World Health Organization

CHAPTER 1

Introduction

You can use this workbook to help you to take the decisions for an e-health strategy and identify the policy issues that you need to address. It is best to use it in workshops with a team of people from many different backgrounds, such as senior civil servants responsible for health, healthcare, information and communications technology (ICT) and finance, doctors, nurses, healthcare managers, ICT managers and ICT suppliers. A team like this often has different views and ideas and using the workbook can help to put these together.

You can use the workbook in many different ways. You can use it as a checklist for the team's agenda and topics. You can use the parts that are most important to you, and you can change and add to the templates so they fit your precise needs better. The templates are in Microsoft Word, so they are easy to modify.

Because e-health is a core resource for healthcare systems, every country needs good policies, strategies and plans for ICT and the associated organisational changes that support improvements in health and healthcare. E-health is this combination of ICT and organisational change. It is not a single project with a fixed timescale and permanent solution. The effort and investment needed has many parts; it is complex, it changes constantly and it is continuous. That is why this workbook covers so many topics.

The main e-health activities included in the workbook are:

- Providing the information needed, when and by whom to support health and healthcare delivery, strategies and services
- Implementing the ICT needed to capture and deliver the information
- Changing the clinical and working practices needed to realise the benefits.

The Commonwealth Health Ministers Meeting (CHMM) in May 2008 agreed to hold high-level meetings between ministers of health and ministers for ICT so they could:

- Identify regional priorities and challenges
- Foster strategic partnerships
- Reach a consensus on e-health projects in selected countries
- Promote the exchange of information on e-health expertise.

The first high-level meeting was in the Seychelles for ministers in the East, Central and Southern African Health Community (ECSA) in September and October 2008. Ministers and their colleagues identified the need for a methodology and templates to help with e-health policies and strategies. The topics are consistent with this, and with the findings from the second high-level dialogues for West Africa in Nigeria in December 2009. They are:

- Develop user-friendly and comprehensive e-health policies and strategies and projects
- Develop a step-by-step approach to develop e-health policies, strategies and projects with minimal external assistance
- Identify the information that may not be readily available and needs collecting to complete e-health policies, strategies and projects.

The workbook disaggregates the themes and complexities of e-health so you can deal with each of these topics separately and link them back together. Then assessments and decisions can follow through in a continuous loop. A separate workbook is available to help you to describe e-health proposals to secure finance. A third workbook came out of the ECSA ministers' second initiative, which set up an e-health working group to develop a generic questionnaire for you to use to identify and assess the current e-health situation.

This workbook's content also draws from the e-health experiences of the World Health Organization (WHO), the Bellagio Conference on e-health, the European Union (EU), selected countries in the ECSA and the West Africa Health Organisation (WAHO) regions and other Commonwealth countries. These have several common themes that you can adopt. However, differences between member states may be more important than these similarities, so it is important that your e-health polices and strategies reflect the realities of your country and organisation. The workbook aims to bridge this gap by helping you to build from your current efforts, knowledge, experience and initiatives to:

- Identify and share the lessons and challenges, and learn from each other
- Identify practical steps to achieve each country's e-health goals
- Identify the stakeholders and their approaches to engagement in e-health.

E-health policies and strategies must be one of the topics of your country's overall health and healthcare strategies. You can use the workbook to show how e-health fits in. You must also integrate e-health with strategies for social and economic development and reflect the nature of your country's health economies, especially where there is a mix of public, private, faith-based organisations (FBOs), non-governmental organisations (NGOs) and charities delivering healthcare services. E-health policies and strategies in these mixed health economies are demanding to prepare. Dealing with the situation successfully will help you to be clear about the costs and benefits that can be realised by each type of healthcare organisation from each e-health project, and so will help to direct the required e-health investment.

When you use the workbook, you must also reflect the dynamic context of e-health. The templates are not a set of forms that you can complete in one go. Opportunities, policies, strategies and projects are always changing and developing, so you can change the workbook to reflect these developments.

CHAPTER 2

Using the Methodology and Templates

The workbook gives you a structure to use in workshops that bring people together from a wide range of interests. Workshop participants may include:

- Ministers and senior officials responsible for health and technology
- Healthcare professionals, especially doctors, nurses and pharmacists
- Healthcare leaders and managers
- Healthcare ICT professionals
- FBOs
- NGOs
- ICT and telecommunications vendors.

Important material that you may want to refer to before and during the workshops includes current strategies and plans for:

- Improving health
- Strengthening healthcare
- General ICT investment
- ICT specific to health and healthcare
- E-health finance and affordability.

Documents dealing with these can provide some of the information you need to take the decisions for e-health policies and strategies. The workbook helps you to structure these decisions: you should use it as a framework, not as a set of forms that you have to fill in. Some parts of the workbook may not be directly relevant for your country, so you can ignore or change these as you see fit. However, in doing so it is important to elicit a wide range of perspectives on e-health with your colleagues. At each workshop you may want to conclude with agreements on the next steps for e-health polices and strategies, and specify the work necessary to develop those steps for review at subsequent meetings.

A brief commentary introduces each chapter of the workbook. You can add the specific needs and issues of your country to these commentaries during your workshops.

CHAPTER 3
An International Perspective

Many international organisations have dealt with the different aspects of e-health. You may find it helpful to refer to these before you use your workbook. Three international e-health perspectives have come from the World Health Organization (WHO), the Bellagio Conference and the European Union (EU).

WHO Building Foundations for E-Health identifies many initiatives to support countries' e-health policies and strategies. Examples are:

- *Connecting for Health: Global Vision, Local Insight* (WHO, 2005)
- *Electronic Health Records: Manual for Developing Countries* (WHO, 2006a)
- *Everybody's Business: Strengthening Health Systems to Improve Health Outcomes* (WHO, 2007)
- *eHealth Tools and Services: Needs of the Member States* (WHO, 2006b)

Taken together, these show the vast range and complexity of e-health, and indicate the need to compile policies and strategies in way that is practical, flexible and relevant to your country's needs. A core theme is building capacity for e-health.

Bellagio E-Health Call to Action came from the Rockefeller Foundation conference on e-health (RF, 2008). It has a vision and goal for better health for everyone by using interoperable e-health. Three core themes are that:

- Human capacity building is essential in using e-health systems and technical support
- Emerging infrastructure and e-health present a window of opportunity to foster interoperability across geographies, technologies and programmes
- Systems should be person-centred and emphasise strengthening people's health and health systems.

The EU e-Health Action Plan is taking longer than expected to achieve its objectives. This provides a valuable lesson. It reveals the challenges, complexities and timescales of e-health, and it is essential that you reflect these realities in your countries' e-health policies and strategies. There have been several EC initiatives to realise its action plan, such as identifying and promulgating the net benefits of e-health (EC, 2007 and EC, 2009a) and seeking financing opportunities to boost e-health investment (EC, 2009b). An important finding from the financing e-health study is that the biggest barrier to investment is lack of capacity: people do not have the skills and knowledge required, especially in order to take effective decisions for e-health. This is broadly consistent with the position identified by the East and West Africa High-Level E-Health Dialogues. Improving this position must be a core part of your country's e-health policies and strategies.

Table 1. Simple comparison of three international contributions to e-health development

E-health policy and strategy topic	*Building Foundations for eHealth (WHO, 2006c)*	*Bellagio E-Health Call to Action 2008 (RF, 2008)*	*EU e-Health Action Plan 2004 (CEC, 2004)*	*Relevance to my country's e-health policies and strategies*	*Notes*
Y = Yes, included; N = No, not included; P = included partially; I = implicit					
ICT	Y	Y	Y		
Organisational change	N	N	Y		
Integration with health strategy	N	N	N		
Leadership	P	Y	Y		
Benefits focus	Y I	Y I	Y I		
Benefits realisation	N	N	N		
Engagement	N	N	N		
Investment plan	N	N	Y		
Affordability	Y	N	N		
Interoperability	Y	Y	Y		
Functionality	N	N	N		
Usability	N	N	Y		
Architecture	N	Y	N		
Infrastructure	Y	Y	Y		
Procurement	Y	N	N		
Implementation	P	N	Y		
Programme management	N	N	N		
Project management	Y	N	N		
Training and capacity	Y	Y	N		
E-health investment risk	N	N	N		
Informatics	Y	P	N		
Identifiers	N	N	Y		
Standards	P	P	P		
Confidentiality	Y	N	Y		
Security	Y	N	Y		
Legal	Y	N	Y		
Realistic timescales	N	N	N		

Table 1 shows a simple comparison of the three perspectives. It has a column for you to make notes about the relevance for your work.

Core themes

The three e-health perspectives in Table 1 have different strategic emphases, but they offer a shared big picture for countries' e-health policies and strategies. Chart 1 shows some of the main themes and their links as part of an integrated e-health strategy loop.

Chart 1. Main themes for e-health policies and strategies and their links

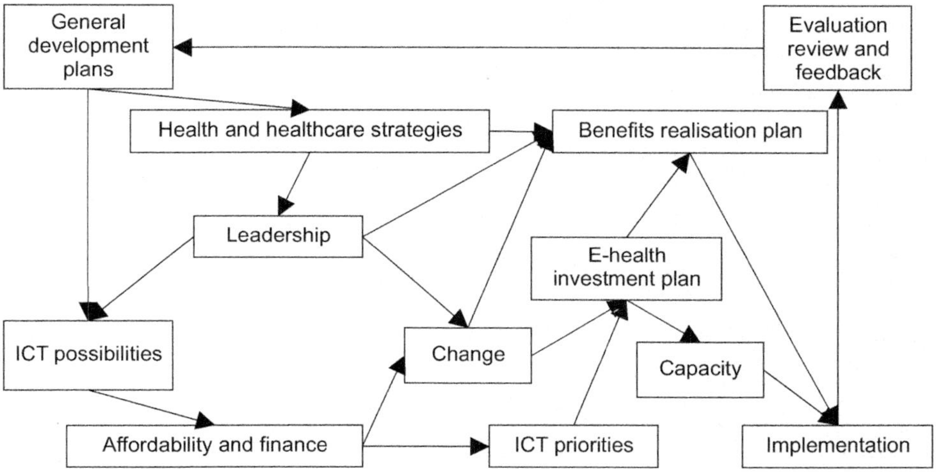

Table 2. Questions and answers on the main policy themes

Questions for you	*Answers*
Which topics in Chart 1 do you already have in place? Which topics do you need to do more about? Which topics are the most important for your work?	

You need your colleagues to work with you to identify and link the dependencies in the loop that enable each e-health project to contribute to achieving the goals of your country's health strategy. Chart 2 shows a simplified, generic connection of interdependencies for each e-health project selected as part of the e-health investment plan.

Chart 2. Illustrative simplified connection between factors for successful e-health

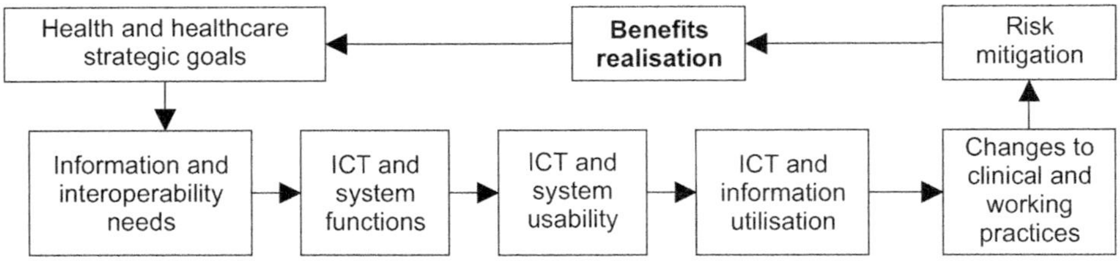

The remainder of the workbook deals with each of the topics in Charts 1 and 2. The templates help to identify, quantify and link affordable e-health themes to reflect each country's e-health strategy.

Table 3. Questions and answers on successful e-health

Questions for you	*Answers*
Which topics in Chart 2 do you already have in place?	
Which topics do you need to do more about?	
Which topics are the most important for your work?	

Benchmarking

In addition to information from the international sources in Table 1, you may want to benchmark your position against equivalent countries and organisations. It could be between ministries, hospitals and districts. Examples of benchmark topics are:

- E-health policies and strategies, including interoperability standards, confidentiality and security
- E-health investment plans
- Types of e-health projects, including performance and costs
- Engagement with patients and patient groups
- Engagement with healthcare professionals
- Partnerships with ICT vendors, donors and civil society
- Procurement arrangements
- Project management
- Capacity initiatives

- Changes to clinical and working practices in place
- Costs over the whole lifecycle
- Benefits realised for all stakeholders, including citizens and patients, healthcare professionals, healthcare provider organisations and third parties
- Risks encountered, avoided and mitigated.

Successful e-health benchmarking needs information and analysis of current investment and service provision and performance completed before benchmark data is used. It is essential to identify the reasons for the good performance of your service and the services that you are using as a benchmark. Benchmarking can be time consuming to complete, and relies on effective partnerships and collaboration between all parties involved. These are challenging to set up, so you if you want to benchmark you may want to wait until you have a draft e-health strategy that you can use as one of the information sources.

CHAPTER 4
Country Social and Economic Development Plans

Countries' plans for social and economic development include expanding ICT infrastructure to support services such as the internet, broadband and mobile phones. For example, Kenya, Tanzania and Uganda are laying fibre optic cable across their countries as part of an international communication project that is laying cable under the Indian Ocean. In Bangladesh, the government is expanding the availability of broadband as part of its policy initiatives to stimulate economic opportunities. These types of projects provide opportunities for e-health piloting and scalability to a wider base of users. Table 4 provides examples of different types of ICT development.

Table 4. Examples of general development initiatives and their links to e-health

General development theme	*Initiative*	*E-health opportunity*	*Potential for e-health strategy*	*Opportunities for e-health policies and strategies*
Expansion of mobile phone networks	ICT suppliers	Communications between patients and professionals	Invest in disseminating health and healthcare data to patients	
Expansion of NGO activities	Provide impregnated nets to reduce incidence of malaria	Logistics and drugs information systems to support distribution	Invest in logistics systems to support NGOs	
Availability of health networks	Africa Health Infoway (AHI)	Expanded access to health and healthcare information for hospitals, districts and communities	Invest in access to healthcare, diagnosis, treatments, standards, health surveillance and health information	
Availability of Internet, broadband and mobile phones to support local communities	Expanding local small businesses	Increase demand for local access to broadband services	Take advantage of expanded communication networks for exchange of health and healthcare data	

These developments can also offer opportunities for healthcare organisations to share the costs of communication networks as part of affordable, long-term e-health strategies. It is consistent with the WHO perspective (WHO, 2007) that the Millennium Development Goals (MDGs) need:

- Increased investment in health systems and services
- Improvements in the performance of existing healthcare resources
- New ways to harness communities, NGOs and the private sector
- Specific initiatives in order to benefit the poor.

Success will be limited unless other sectors of the economy contribute to better health, such as expanding local business opportunities, increasing employment, reducing poverty and producing more food. E-health has to be part of this approach. ICT suppliers already provide a wide range of services to developing countries, and forecasts are that these will expand (Scott *et al.*, 2004). Increasing e-health capacity should rely as much as possible on the expansion of general infrastructure. In turn, e-health will increase the demand for ICT infrastructure and in so doing will contribute to general development. In this context, e-health plans and projects must integrate with initiatives of those ministries dealing with ICT and other technologies.

Table 5. Questions and answers on general ICT plans

Questions for you	*Answers*
Who can tell you more about your country's plans for general ICT development?	
What are the opportunities for e-health to link in to them?	
Which opportunities are the most important for your work?	

International e-health initiatives may also be relevant for countries' e-health strategies. The Africa Health Infoway (AHI) invests in 53 countries, enabling access to health and healthcare data for several hospitals and communities. This type of initiative can have a direct impact on e-health strategies.

Table 6. Questions and answers on Africa Health Infoway

Questions for you	*Answers*
What do you know about your country's links with the Africa Health Infoway?	
What are the opportunities for e-health to link into it?	
Which opportunities are the most important for your work?	

Your e-health strategies and plans must recognise that resources for e-health are scarce. Healthcare spending by governments in developing countries has increased steadily, but moderately, by about 0.5 per cent a year since the late 1990s (Goldsbrough *et al.*, 2007). This has largely reversed the decline in the mid-1990s, but spending has levelled off at about 2.5 per cent of gross domestic product (GDP). It represents about 6.5 per cent of government spending, again correcting a decline in the mid-1990s. Adding private spending on healthcare increases average spending to about 5.5 per cent of GDP. There is also a wide range of healthcare spending in developing countries: for example, the range is from Nigeria's government spending of less than 0.5 per cent of GDP in 2005 compared to Malawi's spending of about 37 per cent. However, changing this perspective for the value of GDP and the population, government healthcare spending for each person shows a different view. Nigeria is much closer to Malawi's spending, both below US$25 per person per year, dropping Malawi to the bottom half of the ranking. Seychelles has the largest spending among developing countries – about US$425 annually for each person. These findings confirm that e-health spending must be specifically targeted and carry low risks that are strictly mitigated.

These generalisations may not be helpful to you in planning your specific e-health investment. You will need to know more about the amount of money that your country has planned for healthcare and e-health spending over the next few years. This may not be available. A medium-term financial plan may not have been established as yet.

CHAPTER 5

Health and Healthcare Policies and Strategies for E-Health

Health and healthcare strategies and plans should look about five years ahead to:

- Increase equitable access to health services
- Improve service quality and responsiveness
- Improve efficiency and effectiveness
- Foster partnerships to improve health and healthcare delivery
- Improve healthcare financing.

These goals help to specify the outcomes that are required, the investment needed to achieve those outcomes and their relative priorities, and they can help you to identify achievable action plans for e-health. For example, improving access to healthcare may need more qualified and trained health workers with new ideas. E-health projects, such as telemedicine and e-learning, can help with this goal, so could be part of your e-health strategy. These types of projects may help to strengthen team working in healthcare delivery. Developing ICT infrastructure and capacity may also be essential to support these types of e-health initiatives.

Health ministries can take on an advocacy role in e-health by engaging with all types of stakeholders, especially through awareness campaigns and information sharing. These actions could describe a government's long-term plans to connect all health and healthcare activities and documents, extending from patients' appointments to public health exercises such as disease surveillance. These links are important so that e-health investment can fit into your country's overall health strategy, a concept sometimes called 'mainstreaming e-health'. Such mainstreaming is essential in setting the benefits to be gained from e-health and avoiding wasted investment with no, few or low-priority benefits. During the workshops, you and your colleagues should identify the benefits and objectives of e-health as part of the overall investment.

As a guide, Table 7 sets out some questions and some examples of answers for you to use as prompts to come up with your own answers. You will probably have to ask more specific questions than these to complete your e-health polices and strategies.

Your answers will provide you with the basis for the desired benefits. These in turn should drive your e-health policies, strategies and plans. They assemble into a simple template shown as Table 8.1. The information is complex and sophisticated, as it fans out across the columns as the number of answers increase. Table 8.2 is for you to expand by inserting the relevant rows from Table 8.1 below, and by changing the columns too if you want a different emphasis. You can then prepare a draft example using your country's health strategy to use with your colleagues in workshops.

This analysis identifies and connects the information needs and priorities of strategic health and healthcare initiatives, the benefits and the beneficiaries. This is essential information for successful e-health. Where information in the table is unclear, this can reveal the need to improve health and healthcare policies and strategies before e-health investment should proceed.

Table 7. Examples of links to health strategies

Some requirements from health policies and strategies	*Examples of answers and information needed*	*Your answers*
What are the high-priority diseases and conditions in communities?	Responding to high-priority diseases such as HIV/AIDS, malaria and tuberculosis as part of the MDG initiatives should include identifying the clinical, operational and management information and benefits needed from e-health.	
What is the plan to prevent ill health and promote good health?	Activities that prevent or reduce the incidence of diseases and conditions, including avoidable maternal deaths, epidemics and new diseases, should include identifying the public health information and benefits needed from e-health.	
What is planned to improve the quality of and access to healthcare and related services?	Initiatives such as improved patient safety, streamlined care and services available for communities previously denied them. all need clinical, operational and management information.	
What is planned to improve the efficiency of healthcare resources and activities?	Cutting waste by improving supply chains for drugs and medical and surgical supplies should include identifying the information needed in this respect.	
What are the planned links to social care, education, FBO and NGO activities?	Services that integrate with healthcare, such as aid, social workers, schools and housing, and provided by public and private entities and NGOs need to share information.	
What are the priorities for general investment and expansion in healthcare and other resources and activities?	Extra doctors, more nurses and midwives, more pharmacists, more drugs, more medical and surgical supplies, more clinics and more hospitals all increase demand for information to be help to achieve objectives.	
What are the links to general development initiatives?	Improving education, business and economic activity in communities can have requirements that integrate with health and healthcare activities.	

Some requirements from health policies and strategies	*Examples of answers and information needed*	*Your answers*
Who are the stakeholders and beneficiaries of e-health?	Citizens, patients, carers, doctors, nurses, midwives, therapists, pharmacists, healthcare support staff, healthcare provider organisations, FBOs, NGOs, charities, healthcare suppliers and third party payers.	
What are the different health goals and resources for short-term, medium-term and long-term horizons?	A short-term goal could be expanding ICT capacity; a goal for the medium term could be improved departmental information; and a long-term health goal could be individual patient records.	
What are the requirements and developments needed to e-health to support these health goals?	For example: generic communication networks, information and ICT standards and policies, telehealth and telemedicine, computerised physician order entry (CPOE), picture archiving and communications systems (PACS), e-prescribing, electronic patient records (EPR), radio frequency identification (RFID), shared information between appropriate healthcare professionals for health surveillance and direct patient care, health information for citizens, changes in clinical and working practices.	

Table 8.1 Illustrative requirements and benefits from health and healthcare strategies for e-health strategies

Key requirements from health and healthcare policies and strategies	*Information needed for health policies and strategies*	*Information priorities for health policies and strategies*	*Benefits and beneficiaries*
Reduce child mortality	Vaccination	Recording	Knowledge for nursesFewer children at risk
		Scheduling	Knowledge for nursesFewer children at risk
		Supply chain	Knowledge for nurses, efficient supply, nurses supported Fewer children at risk
	Community case mix	Patient locations	Knowledge for nurses, children, families and nurses
		Patient conditions	Knowledge for nurses, children, families and nurses
		Care plans	Knowledge for nurses, children, families and nurses
	Nutrition programmes	Supply chain	Knowledge for nurses, children, families, nurses, NGOs and suppliers
	Information for citizens	Knowledge bases across public networks	Knowledge for citizens, patients, carers, communities and vulnerable groups
	Medical records	Recent conditions, diagnoses and treatments	Knowledge for professionals, children, families, doctors and nurses
Improve maternal health			
Combat HIV/AIDS			
Combat malaria			
Combat tuberculosis			
Improve access to services			
Strengthen quality management			
Enhance ministry regulation			
Enhance health research			
Support scientific, diagnostic, analytic and forensic services			
Co-ordinate continuing medical education (CME) and continuing professional development (CPD)			
Legal changes for policies	Confidentiality	Integrated legislation for a unified health sector	
	Security		
Unique citizen identifiers	National unique codes	EPR and national and regional access	Compile all health information into unique records
Capacity building	ICT infrastructures	Integrate with expanded public networks	Cost sharing
	Training		

Table 8.2 Actual requirements and benefits from the country's health and healthcare strategies for the e-health strategy

Key requirements from health and healthcare policies and strategies	*Information needed for health policies and strategies*	*Information priorities for the health policies and strategy*	*Benefits and beneficiaries*

It is essential to engage effectively with doctors and other healthcare professionals and their professional groups from the start of e-health strategies and projects. E-health can have a significant effect on the way they work. Some people see ICT (Yunkap Kwankam and Richardson, 2007) as the 'third pillar' of the healthcare sector. The first was chemistry in the nineteenth century, which led to the pharmaceuticals industry. The second was physics in the twentieth century, which created imaging systems. This idea of the third pillar is consistent with the findings from e-health impact studies (Stroetmann et al., 2006), which show that e-health is an investment in the resources for healthcare professionals. It helps them to improve the services they provide, and so benefits patients and communities directly. These are similar to the goals for increasing the healthcare professional workforce, new drugs, new medical and scientific technologies and health initiatives such as nutrition programmes. From this perspective, the right types of e-health are essential tools to provide information and knowledge for doctors and other healthcare professionals.

Patients are often keen to engage with the health service through information and communications technologies to help to reduce the intrusion of health services on their lives. Explaining these new opportunities to patients often leads to positive responses. Hence, effective engagement with patients and patient groups about e-health plans and projects is essential to success. There are several ways that you can approach this.

In Scotland, the health service sent a leaflet to every household to advise and consult on changes proposed for the Emergency Care Summary (Dobrev *et al.*, 2009). It also engaged nationally with patient groups from the outset of the project. Other arrangements that you may consider are to link with patients directly at each healthcare facility. Here, professionals can advise patients about e-health proposals. Their collective ideas and concerns will form valuable contributions to collect and transfer into the projects. These discussions must be part of the e-health project and consistently organised, not just general conversations. Patients in each location must have consistent information about the e-health initiatives and be able to offer comments freely. Common topics are data confidentiality and security. They may also want to know how the e-health project will benefit them, their families and communities, especially where patients are direct users, as with e-health projects that provide web-based access to health information and services. It is a good idea to let patients know what has happened to their contributions, as this is courteous and reinforces their role.

Good e-health policies are also essential for success. However, there is a dilemma. It is extremely challenging to compile effective e-health policies in the absence of e-health, due to the lack of practical details. Without e-health in place, some policies can be rather theoretical, excessive and may even constrain progress on e-health. As a result, policies developed in parallel with the e-health strategy and projects are sometimes better. However, you will need a step-by-step approach to e-health so that policies do not fall too far behind. Examples of policy topics for e-health identified during e-health workshops could include:

- Confidentiality
- Security
- Unique national patient numbers
- A national patient master index
- Technical interoperability:
    - o Procuring open source systems
    - o Procuring web-based systems
- Semantic interoperability, such as Health Level (HL) 2 to HL 7, for interoperability standards of electronic interchange of clinical, financial and administrative information between computer systems used in healthcare
- Clinical coding, such as the WHO's International Statistical Classification of Diseases (ICD) and Related Health Problems (10th Revision Version) and the Systematised Nomenclature of Medicine Clinical Terms (SNOMED)
- Procurement and partnerships
- Capacity building.

You can start work on these topics immediately with a single, or a few, working groups integrated into your e-health initiative. The working groups could report to your workshops, so you colleagues can discuss the ideas, options and proposals before the final versions are included in the e-health policies and strategy documents. Proposal finalisation should take place after engagement with appropriate stakeholders as part of sustained stakeholder relationships.

CHAPTER 6

Leadership and Collaboration

The attributes of leaders have been summarised by two gurus as follows:

- 'Management is doing things right; leadership is doing the right things' – Peter F Drucker
- 'Management is about arranging and telling; leadership is about nurturing and enhancing' – Tom Peters.

You need these distinctions between leadership and management in place for e-health to succeed. An example from e-health is that leaders should lead the e-health programme; managers should manage the projects. An e-health programme takes forward the whole e-health strategy for ICT and change, and identifies the clinical and executive leaders and the individual leader, sometimes called 'the owner', directly responsible. Programmes co-ordinate and organise several e-health projects, so are more complicated than projects. Programmes have longer timescales than individual projects. A programme focus is to realise the benefits, whereas projects focus on outputs. You can use Table 9 to identify the differences between your programmes and projects.

Table 9. Examples of the differences between programmes and projects

Programme board	*Project board*
Benefits	**Outputs**
Deals with several projects	Deals with one project
Wider strategic benefits	Explicit, scoped deliverables
Benefits realised during and after projects	Benefits realised after completion
Change and transformation of clinical and working practices, teams and organisations	
What is the role of your e-health programme board?	**What is the role of your project boards?**

Who are the leaders you need as members of your programme board?

Other questions you need to answer are: Who should your leaders lead? and What skills, knowledge and experience do they need to lead?

Who are the leaders?

Three main types of leaders are needed: clinical, executive and political. Political leaders formulate policy, decide on appropriate legal and financial frameworks, and then ensure that they are implemented effectively. Their role extends to monitoring and evaluating progress. This knowledge enables them to advocate e-health initiatives. Effective clinical leaders know a great deal about medicine, health organisations and e-health, sometimes with formal qualifications in both medicine and aspects of ICT. Clinical leaders make sure that e-health programmes avoid imposing and exhorting, instead relying on participation and collaboration. Executive leaders have experience in business strategy, operational management, change management, ICT and investment decisions.

Leaders' roles derive from their personal attributes, not their job descriptions. These roles are not the same as leads, such as the clinical leads needed for e-health projects and project management teams. They can be the same people, but a leadership role needed to develop healthcare is not the same as the narrower lead role needed for each e-health project, although it is important that project leads also have leadership skills.

Who should they lead?

At its simplest, leaders should lead all the stakeholders and managers affected by e-health. Clinical leaders have a specific role too. They should lead the healthcare professionals affected by thee-health proposal, and make sure that projects meet their requirements effectively. This is effective engagement, and places responsibilities on clinical leaders to gain commitment for choices and decisions, and so subsequent benefits realisation. Executive leaders should lead the arrangements for effective engagement with all stakeholders and partnerships. They should also ensure that an effective balance between competing aims is set and sustained. This extends to leading teams in excellent decision-taking, especially fixing things that have gone wrong and avoiding or navigating potential ICT and system crashes.

What skills and knowledge do they need to lead?

Clinical and executive leaders are complementary, and comprise a leadership team. They need effective listening skills to make this work. Listening is also crucial in effective stakeholder engagement. They must make sure that projects have effective and sustainable enablers in place for people to succeed with e-health investment, and they must minimise or remove inhibitors to success. Other traits include:

- Sustaining relationships with all types of stakeholders
- Identifying choices
- Taking e-health investment decisions
- Change management
- Managing and mitigating risk
- Seeking ICT possibilities and opportunities.

Effective leaders rely on two main sources. One is their own experience. The other is their capacity for continuous learning, which can be more important for success. Continuous learning is from other organisations as well as the leader's own, and needs an open, sharing approach to e-health. Such learning also derives from their grasp of the changing potential of ICT for organisations, and the arrangements needed to realise this. A common thread running through leadership is that good leaders always know that they need to know more, and will go and find that knowledge. They never believe that they know all they need to know. Assessing the status of leadership for e-health helps to identify the need to develop leadership as part of the e-health strategy. Table 10 illustrates a possible way for you to assess leadership.

Collaboration

E-health rarely, if ever, succeeds without collaboration. Achieving this needs successful engagement with all relevant stakeholders. Collaboration is time consuming, and leaders need to be part of a team with stakeholders to agree ways to meet their e-health needs. It differs from consultation, where it may be possible to disregard or dilute responses. Engagement requires collaboration, and leaders need to respond constructively, not to dilute or disregard. Assessing collaboration capacity is included in the leadership assessment in Table 10.

Political leaders, especially ministers of health and ministers of technology, are crucial in:

- Putting in place and supporting effective clinical and executive leaders and leadership activities
- Supporting collaboration between entities in mixed-health economies
- Creating and sustaining effective collaboration between appropriate ministries
- Integrating e-health and its governance arrangements with other health and healthcare investment, so avoiding the problems of e-health isolation.

These, and other ministerial responsibilities relevant for each country, should be set out in e-health policies and strategies.

Table 10. Illustrative leadership assessment

Who are your political leaders?	*Who are your clinical leaders?*	*Who are your executive leaders?*	*Goals, roles and skills and knowledge needed*	*What skills and knowledge are needed?*	*What extra training and development is needed for e-health leaders?*
			Engagement		
			Partnerships and collaboration		
			Policy and regulatory framework		
			ICT and standards		
			E-health potential		
			Engagement		
			Partnerships and collaboration		
			Policy and regulatory framework		
			ICT and standards		
			E-health potential		
			Programme management		
			Benchmarking		
			Risk management		
			Mixed-health economies		
			Engagement		
			Changing clinical practices		
			Partnerships and collaboration		
			Policy and regulatory framework		
			ICT and standards		
			E-health potential		
			Programme management		
			Risk management		
			Engagement		
			Partnerships and collaboration		
			Policy and regulatory framework		
			ICT and standards		
			E-health potential		
			Programme management		
			Project management		
			Risk management		
			Benchmarking		
			Change management		
			Mixed-health economies		

CHAPTER 7

ICT Possibilities

Effective clinical and executive leaders must know the potential of a wide range of e-health opportunities that can benefit health and healthcare. ICT and organisational change is complex. The boundaries between the two are often blurred, and leaders have to be aware of the current opportunities that they offer. Without this, they will be unable to choose effectively between competing demands.

There are many types of e-health, such as:

- Clinical information systems, such as specialised tools for healthcare professionals in hospitals, primary care and other care settings, including notes and records, test results, order entry and decision support (Amarasingham *et al.*, 2009)
- Telecare, telehealth, telemedicine and m-health systems and services (UNF/VF, undated)
- Integrated regional and national health information networks and distributed electronic health record (EHR) systems and associated services
- Logistics, including supply chain management and resource scheduling
- Non-clinical systems, including systems for health education and health promotion aimed at patients and citizens, specialised systems for researchers, and public health data collection and analysis and support systems for clinical processes not used directly by patients or healthcare professionals
- E-learning, especially undergraduate, post-graduate and continuous professional education
- Billing and healthcare management activities.

This is not a list of separate activities. It may be more helpful to see them as an integrated structure, rather like bricks in a wall. Chart 3.1 provides an example.

Chart 3.1. An example of structured and integrated e-health

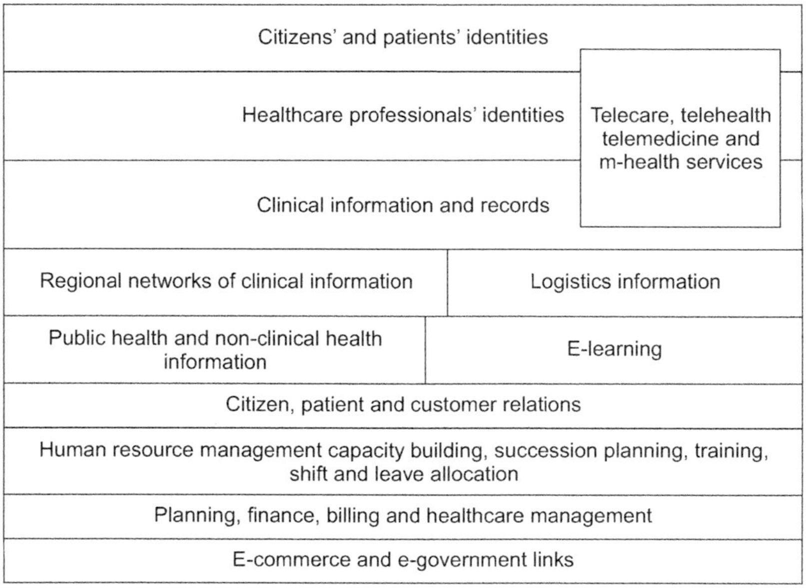

From Chart 3.1, you can compile your own e-health structure to help you put the possible e-health project headings into a hierarchy, ranging from patients and communities through to healthcare management. You can change the shape and structure of the boxes using the text box facility using the tool bar at the bottom of the Word screen.

Chart 3.2. A template for you to compile your integrated e-health structure

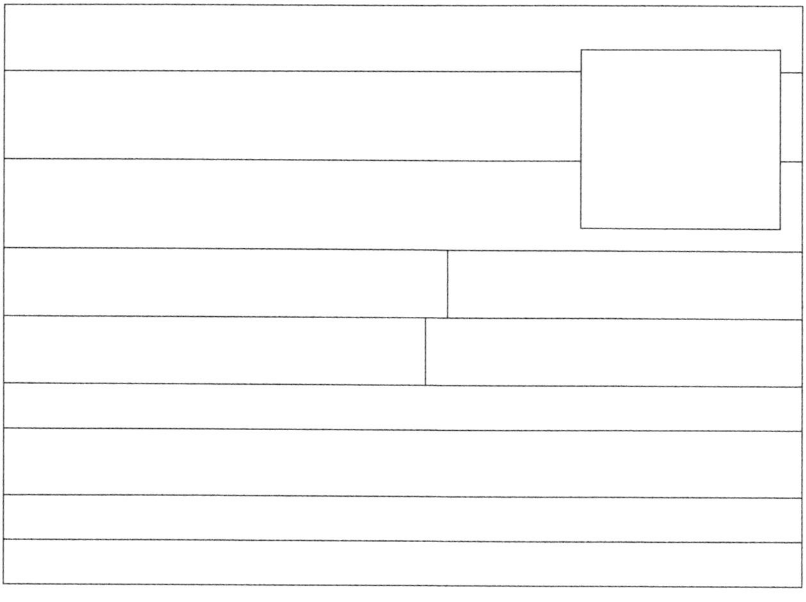

An important feature of these types of ICT possibilities is making sure you assemble them in a way that is relevant to the health and healthcare perspectives of your e-health policy-makers and strategists. There is no right or wrong way to do this. The main goal is to set out the possibilities in a way that is reasonably comprehensive. You can then review these with your colleagues in the workshops, and establish your e-health options as a constructive mix of ICT and organisational change. There are numerous combinations, and you need to find one that fits your setting.

In addition to the specific information requirements of health and healthcare, e-health also relies on general ICT services. Some of these may also be available in the general economy, offering the enabling potential of helping with:

- Communications networks
- Architecture
- Interoperability
- Functionality
- Usability
- Capacity
- Coverage, especially for networks
- Informatics, such as data definitions, coding models and identifiers
- Technical and semantic interoperability
- Computers of all types
- Application software
- Middleware
- Analytical tools.

ICT potential is a vast area of knowledge. It changes constantly. You, your workshop colleagues and e-health leaders will find it demanding to keep up with all the information available. Hence, it is likely that dealing with relevant segments will be essential. This supports the need for collaboration between ministries responsible for health, technology development, suppliers and international agencies. It also requires good teamwork between e-health leaders, healthcare professionals, ICT managers in healthcare and ICT suppliers. Table 11 illustrates a possible assessment for you to use.

Table 11. Illustrative assessment of ICT requirements, benefits and costs

E-health types	*ICT application*	*Healthcare area*	*ICT requirements*	*Potential benefits*	*Your estimate of costs, by type*
Clinical	Diagnostic results with computerised physician order entry (CPOE)	Laboratories, outpatients, inpatients and primary care	Capacity, applications and reliable networks (CAN)	Faster access to results, fewer repeat tests, reliable access to patient histories	Payments to ICT suppliers, project management teams, changing clinical and working practices, engagement
	E-prescribing, including decision support	Treatment	CAN	More accurate prescribing and dispensing, sharing information	As above
	Picture archiving and communications system (PACS)	Imaging	CAN	Faster access to results, fewer repeat tests	As above
	Prescribing	Prescribing, dispensing, clinical decision support	CAN	Fewer errors, better use of generic drugs	As above
		Transmission	CAN	Better dispensing	As above
	Health records	Summary	CAN	Healthcare professionals share data	As above
		Detailed	CAN	Supporting healthcare professionals' clinical decisions	As above
	Clinical management	Follow-up	CAN, mobile phones (CAN+MP)	Improve health status and medical outcomes and control costs within current premium rates and continuous quality improvement	As above
	Sharing information		Portable CAN + MP (PCAN+MP)	Improve quality and effectiveness of some 30 per cent of direct healthcare spending	As above
Tele- and m-health	Telemedicine	Outpatients	CAN	Increased patient access, avoided travel costs, time savings	As above
		Emergency care	CAN	Increased patient access, avoided travel costs, time savings	As above

E-health types	*ICT application*	*Healthcare area*	*ICT requirements*	*Potential benefits*	*Your estimate of costs, by type*
	Telehealth	Home monitoring	PCAN+MP	Increased patient access, avoided travel costs, time savings	As above
	M-health	Remote patients	Mobile phones and their networks	Better informed patients and compliance	As above
Networks	District	Hospitals	CAN	Faster decision-taking, continuous quality improvement	As above
		Primary care	CAN	Faster decision-taking, continuous quality improvement	As above
		Communities	PCAN	Faster decision-taking, continuous quality improvement	As above
		All	CAN	Faster decision-taking, continuous quality improvement	As above
	National and regional	Hospitals	CAN	Faster decision-taking, continuous quality improvement	As above
		Primary care	CAN	Faster decision-taking, continuous quality improvement	
		Communities	PCAN	Faster decision-taking, continuous quality improvement	As above
		All	CAN	Faster decision-taking, continuous quality improvement	As above
		Public health	CAN	Reduced risk, faster decision-taking, continuous quality improvement	
Secondary	Managing diseases	Public health	CAN	Reduced risk, faster decision-taking, continuous quality improvement	As above
	Managing new diseases	Public health	CAN	Reduced risk, faster decision-taking, continuous quality improvement	

E-health types	*ICT application*	*Healthcare area*	*ICT requirements*	*Potential benefits*	*Your estimate of costs, by type*
	Health surveillance	Public health	PCAN+MP	Reduced risk, faster response and reduced need for healthcare	As above
	Health promotion	Public health	PCAN+MP	Reduced need for healthcare	
	Health education	Public health	PCAN+MP	Reduced need for healthcare	As above
	Research	Clinical, public health	CAN	Increased use of clinical standards	
e-learning	Clinical practices	Medical and nursing	PCAN	Better quality healthcare	As above
	Undergraduate	Medical and nursing	PCAN	Reduced travel time and costs on training	
	Postgraduate	Medical and nursing	PCAN	Reduced travel time and costs on training	As above
	Continuous	Medical and nursing	PCAN	Reduced travel time and costs on training	As above
	General IT	All health workers	PCAN	Reduced travel time and costs on training and more access	As above
	Project management	Project managers	PCAN	Reduced travel time and costs on training and more access	As above
Logistics	Supply chains	Drugs	PCAN	Efficiency, stock holding, traceability,[1] avoided fraud (Otieno, 2006)	As above
		Medical supplies	PCAN	Efficiency, stock holding, traceability, avoided fraud	
	Theatres	Availability	CAN	Efficiency, reliability, streamlined care	As above
		Sterile supplies	CAN	Efficiency, reliability, streamlined care	

1. GS1 Healthcare presentation. http://www.gs1.org

E-health types	*ICT application*	*Healthcare area*	*ICT requirements*	*Potential benefits*	*Your estimate of costs, by type*
	Beds	Availability	CAN	Efficiency, reliability, streamlined care	As above
Planning	National planning		CAN	More analytical, more comprehensive and faster	
	Regional planning		CAN	More analytical, more comprehensive and faster	
Management	Capacity building	All staff	CAN	Supports all other benefits	
	Staff scheduling	All staff	PCAN + databases	Efficiency	
	Billing	Finance staff	CAN + databases	Efficiency, accuracy	
	Activity	Doctors, nurses, allied health professions, managers	PCAN + databases	Efficiency, knowledge, resource allocation	
	Cost and utilisation	Managers, finance managers	CAN + databases	Efficiency, knowledge, resource allocation	

You will probably find the potential benefits to be the hardest part of this template to deal with. There is little hard knowledge about the potential net socio-economic and health benefits, how long they take to realise and where total benefits exceed the total costs over e-health life cycles. There are three main reasons for this:

- There is rarely any systematic identification, measurement and collection of all costs and benefits for e-health projects
- Net benefits depend on the performance before ICT, and again identification and measurement knowledge is lacking
- Potential benefits depend on organisational change as well as ICT, which is often a separate perspective and variable in e-health.

Consequently, when you assess the ICT possibilities, you will have to rely on knowledge from other places, combined with your best available knowledge of local performance. An example of international knowledge is WHO's publication on EHRs (WHO, 2006a).

Other examples are:

- Toward the Establishment of a European eHealth Research Area[2]
- Canada Health Infoway[3]
- Australia's national e-health strategy[4]
- New Zealand's national e-health strategy – a commentary[5]
- Africa Health Infoway.[6]

2. See: http://www.ehealth-era.org [last accessed 17 July 2010].
3. See: http://www.infoway-inforoute.ca [last accessed 17 July 2010].
4. See: http://www.health.gov.au/internet/main/publishing.nsf/Content/National+Ehealth+Strategy [last accessed 17 July 2010].
5. See: http://www.govis.org.nz/conference2007/presentations/brendan-kelly.ppt
6. See: http://www.who.int/africahealthinfoway/en/index.html [last accessed 20 July 2010]; http://www.who.int/africahealthinfoway/AHI%20Brochure.pdf [last accessed 20 July 2010].

CHAPTER 8

Affordability and Finance

Affordability (Jones *et al.*, 2008) is a big constraint on investment. Rather than wait until e-health policies and strategies are complete to test them for affordability, and then discover that they are unaffordable and need resetting, it is better if you begin affordability and related financing analysis at the outset. You should include extra and redeployed resources from existing activities in your review, and pick a timescale that extends across the whole policy, strategy and e-health lifecycle.

E-health spending must be sustainable over the medium term. Typical ICT spending in a developed country can be about 2 per cent of total healthcare spending (EC ISMDG, 2007) – very roughly about US$55 per person per year. For a developing country, this can be the equivalent of about 25 per cent of current healthcare spending, so is not a realistic option. At the other end of the spectrum, a provision of 2 per cent to 7 per cent of healthcare spending is about US$4 per person for e-health in developing countries. This is not sufficient to make much of a long-term impact across whole countries. However, it may offer a realistic and foreseeable position for a sustainable e-health investment programme that enables affordable projects and capacity building; this in turn can lead to a longer-term, larger-scale e-health investment picture – like a jigsaw.

The financial and economic position of healthcare in developing countries is extremely stringent. Exposing it to risk, waste or delay directly diminishes the value of resources and increases the opportunity costs to other programmes. Consequently, the maximum net benefits from e-health measured as the difference between costs and benefits over time, must be realised over the shortest feasible, but not rushed, timescales. This may require e-health projects that rely on proven and commercially available solutions that only require relatively modest local development and implementation. These may increase the chances of realising net benefits over shorter timescales, so your benefit realisation plans can use the experience of previous users. Proven e-health investments also tend to carry lower risks than projects that need significant local development. However, all e-health carries risks.

In mixed-health economies – where governments, charities, NGOs and private healthcare organisations all operate – affordability is complex. Each healthcare provider in each sector can have affordability challenges to bring an e-health investment to fruition. In this setting, stakeholder engagement should include development of an explicit, integrated affordability and financing plan.

E-health policies directly affect affordability, both adversely and beneficially, and may improve overall, long-term affordability. Examples are:

- Reliance on open source and web-based applications

- Capacity building, especially integrated ICT regional and national communications networks and an expanded technical staff to support open source and web-based applications
- Effective semantic and technical interoperability and interfacing
- Online health management information systems
- Step-by-step implementation.

Affordable financing must be in place for the whole e-health life cycle. These financing arrangements also affect affordability directly, through for example:

- Conditions for loans and repayments
- Conditions for leases
- Public–private partnerships (PPPs)
- Business process outsourcing (BPO)
- Government grants
- Increased budgets by stakeholders
- Commitments to redeploy resources already financed, especially doctors' time
- New healthcare reimbursement tariffs
- Cash released from activities, especially ICT legacy systems.

You may be able to use some of these financing arrangements to convert initial short, high-investment peaks into regular annual payments. Achieving this will almost certainly require you to include the financing and procurement arrangements together, especially where leases and PPPs are used. For example, if you buy ICT solutions directly, they can have high expenditure levels in the earlier years and so have a different affordability and financing profile compared to leasing ICT, where expenditure evens out over several years, but will be higher in the later years.

PPPs are fashionable for ICT. They are often complex, with unclear risks and risk sharing. E-health is a complex activity, and adding complex financing and risk models increases this complexity. As a general principle you may want to avoid complex PPPs in favour of simpler models, where effective partnership between all types of stakeholders is easy to understand and at the core of the e-health projects. Nonetheless, a good example of a simple PPP is where ICT vendors agree to finance the whole cost of development in line with users' requirements, and then provide you with the solution at a monthly or annual fee linked to utilisation. These types of arrangements can be easy for all parties to understand and manage.

Table 12 shows a way for you to assess affordability and potential sources of finance for your e-health projects. You may find this table easier to use if you copy it into a spreadsheet. As with all the tables, you can change this one to match the needs of each of your e-health projects. You can also produce a summary table showing the totals for all your e-health projects.

Table 12. Illustrative assessment of affordability and finance

Finance topic	*Type of finance*	*Year 1 US$*	*Year 2 US$*	*Year 3 US$*	*Year 4 US$*	*Year 5 US$*	*Year 6 US$*	*Year 7 US$*	*Year 8 US$*	*Year 9 US$*	*Year 10 US$*	*Total US$*
Sources of finance												
Government grant	Capital	1,00,000										
	Revenue	500,000	500,000									
Total												
Annual income from better billing	Revenue				100,000	150,000	200,000	200,000	200,000	200,000	200,000	
Total												
Private sources	Leases		1,00,000									
	PPP		1,00,000									
Total												
Internal sources	Capital											
	Revenue											
Total												
Total budget												
Payments for finance												
Leases				100,000	100,000	100,000	100,000	100,000	100,000	100,000	100,000	
PPP				100,000	100,000	100,000	100,000	100,000	100,000	100,000	100,000	
Upgrades and obsolescence								50,000	50,000	50,000	50,000	50,000
Total												
Total budget												

CHAPTER 9
Change

Two themes for change are policy and practice.

Policy change

Chapter 5 shows examples of policy topics that you will need for e-health. You may also need some new policies for healthcare, such as reimbursements for services using telemedicine, and using e-learning for medical and nursing training. You should include these types of new policies in your e-health strategy.

Practical change

Changes in the area of e-health often relate to different clinical and working practices achieved by sharing information. Several activities are essential for success:

- Identifying stakeholders
- Engagement with stakeholders
- Agreeing the information requirements of stakeholders, especially healthcare professionals
- Setting procuring models in place, such as leasing and public–private partnerships (PPPs)
- Programme management
- Project management
- Training
- Culture change and benefits realisation.

These activities can combine into change management programmes, with Australia's national e-health strategy Health Connect[7] serving as an example.

Successful change is extremely demanding to achieve, and involves many stakeholders. The complexity increases where healthcare relies on a mixed market, with even more stakeholders to take into account. Change life cycles are often longer than the ICT life cycle, so your plans may need to say how you will deal with this. Some principles of change are that:

- It begins at the outset, before e-health policies and strategies are considered
- The core goal is to create, develop and sustain an information culture

7. See: http://www.health.gov.au/internet/main/publishing.nsf/Content/EHeath+Healthconnect [last accessed 21 July 2010].

- Engagement sets an obligation on e-health planners to meet the needs of stakeholders, which distinguishes engagement from consultation
- There are several ways of achieving change successfully.

Table 13 is an example of a change model as a matrix, showing the potential links between three main types of change and three main types of benefits.

Table 13. Illustrative change model

		Change model	
Benefits	*Process*	*Organic*	*Strategic*
Quality		Doctors and nurses use new information to change clinical and working practices	Healthcare providers and patients use new information for new activities and initiatives
Access			
Efficiency	Systems re-engineering to improve current processes		

Organic and strategic change can be the most valuable, and the most difficult to achieve. Process change tends to be a focus of ICT in health and healthcare, but may not always offer the best impact on benefits. Table 14 shows a possible analysis.

Table 14. Illustrative assessment of change activities for e-health

Activity	*Volumes*	*Timescales*	*Possibilities*	*Details*
Identify stakeholders	Who, and how many?			
Engagement	Which groups need to be included?	How long for?	Professional groups, citizen groups	Who leads?
Stakeholder requirements	How many people are affected?	How long for?		What are the impacts on stakeholders?
Procurement	Who from?	How long?	Options	Links to financing?
Programme management	How many projects?	How long?	Options	Who leads? Links to governance?
Project management	How many managers are needed?	How long?	Options	How many project groups?
Training	How many people need training?	How long for?	Options	Types of training needed? Types of training available?
Culture change	How many people?	How long for?	New teams?	Strengthened healthcare?
Benefits realisation	Who will contribute to the benefits?	How long for?	Options	Who benefits? What are the benefits? Who realises the benefits?

You can delete the text in the table and add your own analysis to discuss and finalise in the workshops.

CHAPTER 10

A Step-By-Step Approach to Policy Development

Two types of e-health investment are known as 'big bang' and 'step-by-step'. In e-health, big bang is not a good idea. It incurs high costs and carries high risks. A big picture is essential for a step-by-step approach that breaks your activities into short-term, medium-term and long-term timescales. E-health is complicated and inherently high risk, so breaking it down into manageable chunks, or a jigsaw, makes sense. However, the step-by-step approach extends investment timescales, which is also inherently risky, so this form of investment does not reduce risk but acts as a way for you to manage risk. It also helps with affordability by spreading the costs over several years. Inevitably, the step-by-step approach defers the benefits too. It also requires sustainable polices that support the large-scale picture.

Step-by-step's big picture must be clear from the outset, then assembled piece-by-piece by each e-health project. A challenge for you and your colleagues in the workshops is to select the ICT and priorities in a timeframe where implementation takes place in a rational, feasible sequence and according to a plan that matches the affordability and change constraints.

A major advantage of step-by-step policy development is the scope it offers you to identify and engage healthcare stakeholders, and work with them so they are sensitised to the complexities and potential impact of e-health. Step-by-step is more manageable than big bang, so offers more chance of success. Yet the step-by-step approach needs policies to promote scalability and net benefits, both from trials and from e-health functionalities that are specific for services dealing with one disease, such as HIV/AIDS, to services dealing with several diseases and different types of citizens.

CHAPTER 11
ICT Priorities

Having completed an assessment of the strategic requirements, e-health potential and affordability, your focus can shift to choices and decisions about the ICT that should be part of the e-health investment plan. Two main types of ICT priorities support capacity building:

- ICT infrastructure – the technology
- ICT skills – the people.

Projects to improve these will help you to achieve high-benefit, high-impact and affordable e-health. An example is from an AKI presentation to use medical and information technology to:

- Minimise operational and personnel expenses
- Enhance customer service
- Trace and measure outcomes for reporting and strategic decisions
- Integrate patient medical data (Kamunyo, undated).

Reaching this type of position depends on bringing together several factors for decisions around the leadership and collaboration themes in chapter 6. It should reflect the affordable projects that will improve and advance interoperability, ICT and data standards, and health and healthcare applications and activities. It is extremely unlikely that governments will be able to meet all ICT priorities, so choices are inevitable. By bringing together several themes, you can compile a realistic schedule of affordable ICT projects. Core features in terms of being realistic are affordability, interoperability, timing and technical feasibility within the skills available.

The Rockefeller Foundation (2008) produced an example of e-health application priorities from a survey. Some of these may match your ICT priorities. In addition, ICT priorities for general communications networks and infrastructures could be ICT priorities. Chart 4 shows a summary.

Chart 4. E-health challenges identified by Rockefeller Foundation survey

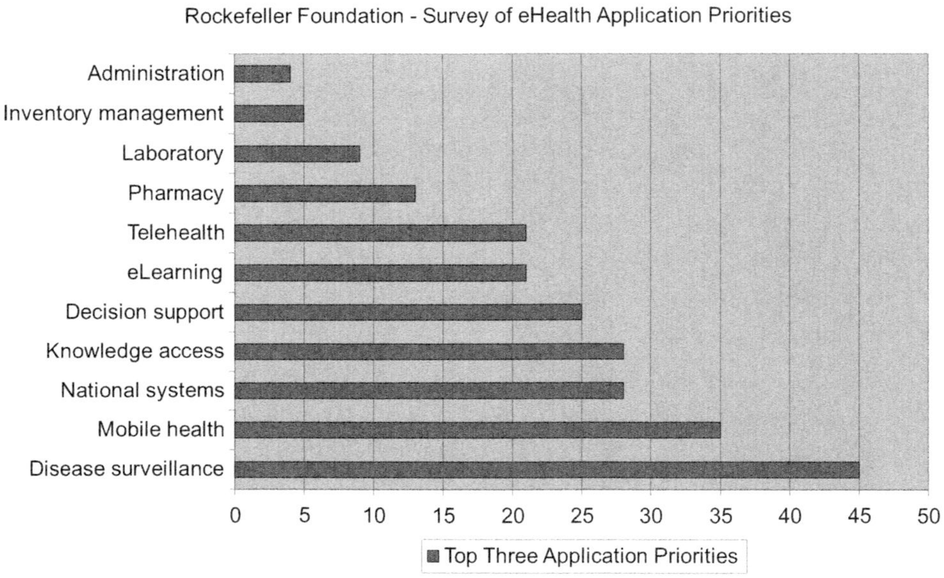

Table 15 shows an approach to compiling a schedule of your ICT priorities. The column 'ICT classification' comprises e-health categories. The column 'ICT requirements' is for general ICT needed to support the applications. You can change all these to fit your needs.

Table 15. Illustrative selection of ICT priorities, requirements, costs and timing for e-health

ICT classification	*ICT application*	*Healthcare area*	*ICT requirements*	*Estimated capital and revenue costs US$*	*Type and year*
Clinical	Diagnostic results	Laboratories			
		Imaging			
	Picture archiving				
	Prescribing	Decision support			
		Transmission			
	Health records	Summary			
		Detailed			
	Clinical management	Beds			
		Theatre			
Tele-	Telemedicine	Outpatients			
		Emergency care			
		Specific conditions			
	Telehealth	Home monitoring			
		Hospital discharge			
	M-health	Patients in communities			
Networks	District	Hospitals			
		Primary care			
		Both			
	National and regional	Hospitals			
		Primary care			
		Both			
		Public health			
Secondary	Public health				
	Health promotion				
	Health education				
	Research				
E-learning	Undergraduate				
	Postgraduate				
	Continuous				
Logistics	Supply chains	Drugs			
		Medical supplies			
	Theatre	Availability			
		Sterile supplies			
	Beds	Availability			
Management	Billing				
	Activity				
	Cost and utilisation				

The relative priorities assigned to each selected ICT investment should reflect the strategic timing need for e-health. Just because ICT is available early in the future, this is not a reflection of its relative strategic priority. Indeed, if you use availability as a criterion, it can distort relative strategic priorities. An example is where many local solutions are available that need to be linked to a national communications network. Is the priority to install the network, then the solutions, or install the solutions first, then the network, or a mix of both? These decisions must reflect the health, healthcare and ICT context, and look for the optimal medium-term outcome over say five years. Your goal is to avoid attractive short-term fixes, but to aim for effective, sustainable longer-term investment with increasing benefits. This is demanding and needs the guidance of your colleagues in the workshops.

CHAPTER 12
E-Health Investment Plan

Realistic e-health investment plans are the product of collaboration between skilled people from the healthcare domain and ICT specialists, so they should be part of your workshops. With these teams in place, the ICT priorities can now switch into an e-health investment plan looking five to ten years ahead. This plan sets out the extra and redeployed resources needed to convert ICT priority decisions into actions and benefits. There are several parts to the core e-health thread, such as:

- Individual e-health projects that comprise the e-health programme of the health and healthcare strategy
- The components of each project
- Realistic timing of deliverables
- ICT and organisational change activities that combine into e-health projects and so the programme
- Fit to the health strategy and investment outcomes
- Spending plan, including the cost of risk
- Human resource plan to deliver and sustain the capacity and capabilities needed for success, especially training for all the skills needed.

Information about the current ICT already in place, its functionalities, its performance and any potential spare capacity is an essential part of an e-health investment plan. The ECSA E-Health Working Group produced a questionnaire to help with this (Commonwealth Secretariat, 2009a). The information ensures that existing capacity and facilities are utilised fully and effectively, before new projects and investment begin.

The e-health thread running through these will help you to match affordability and finance to e-health projects over time. Table 16 is an example of the main themes of an e-health investment plan. Each e-health project should show an indicative description of its costs, benefits and risks over its estimated life cycle to reinforce the realistic, forecast performance. This provides essential information for project management teams and evaluation during the operational stage of the life cycle.

If you publish an e-health roadmap of proposed e-health investment at this step in the loop, it will help to inform citizens and health workers of the ministry's e-health intentions, and the steps it proposes to reach its goals. Some of the information in the template can convert into an e-health road map. The timing of the projects, the human resource plan and capacity plan provide an example. There are two types of roadmap. One deals with the steps needed to move from the e-health strategy to the first e-health project. It includes the arrangements to start engagement with core stakeholders, especially healthcare professionals, and the need to submit proposals to secure finance for the e-health projects. The second type of road map provides the steps to implement a programme of e-health that changes healthcare. Table 16 shows a way for you to schedule these.

Table 16 incorporates many perspectives. You should use these as a simple checklist and redesign a table that matches your situation.

Table 16. Illustrative components of an e-health investment plan

Investment activity	*Components and timing*
Programme	
Project 1	
Project 2	
Project 3	
Project 4 etc.	
Projects	
Stakeholders	
Engagement	
Requirements	
Architecture	
Interoperability	
Functionality	
Applications	
Usability	
Utilisation	
Procurement	
Project management	
Training	
Change	
Benefits realisation	
ICT hardware	
ICT software	
ICT middleware	
ICT other	
Others	
Skills and knowledge from the capacity actions	
Specific local features and content	
Fit to health strategy	
Enablers	
Affordability	
Financing	
Life cycles	

Investment activity	*Components and timing*			
Timescales				
Resources – new				
Resources – redeployed				
Investment outcomes				
Health strategy				
Healthcare strategy				
Development strategy				
General ICT strategy				
Spending plan				
Years	**1**	**2**	**3**	**4 etc.**
Capital outlay				
Revenue outlay				
Capital finance				
Revenue finance				
Financing sources				
Differences				
Capital				
Revenue				
Risk adjusted				
Capital				
Revenue				
Human resource plan				
Extra capacity				
Leaders				
ICT skills				
Programme managers				
Project managers				
Change managers				
Trainers				
Training				
Developed capacity				
Leaders				
ICT skills				
Programme managers				
Project managers				
Change managers				
Trainers				
Medical				
Nursing				
Other healthcare professionals				

There are two main types of resources for e-health investment plans: new and redeployed. New resources can be extra staff and support from ICT suppliers and consultants. The main requirement for new resources is during the earlier stages of e-health investment. Redeployed resources include staff time allocated to e-health activities, especially engagement and training. They also include the saving from legacy systems that terminate when new e-health investment comes on line. These can be substantial when e-health replaces manual systems.

Three main e-health benefits are quality, access or efficiency. They accrue to a wide range of stakeholders, including:

- Citizens
- Healthcare professionals and other workers
- Healthcare provider organisations of all types in mixed-health economies
- Third party healthcare organisations, such as third party payers and charities
- NGOs and development communities and projects
- Other government agencies.

These benefits result in a net benefit as a socio-economic return (SOR) that extends well beyond the cash gains, if any, of returns on investment (ROI). However, these are specialised analyses that you need not attempt at this stage. You may find it helpful to identify and describe the main features of each e-health project, such as how long it takes for the ICT stages and when the benefits realisation activities can start. Benefits for stakeholders from an e-health project can have a curve as shown in Chart 5.

Chart 5. Illustrative cost, benefit and net benefit curves for an e-health project

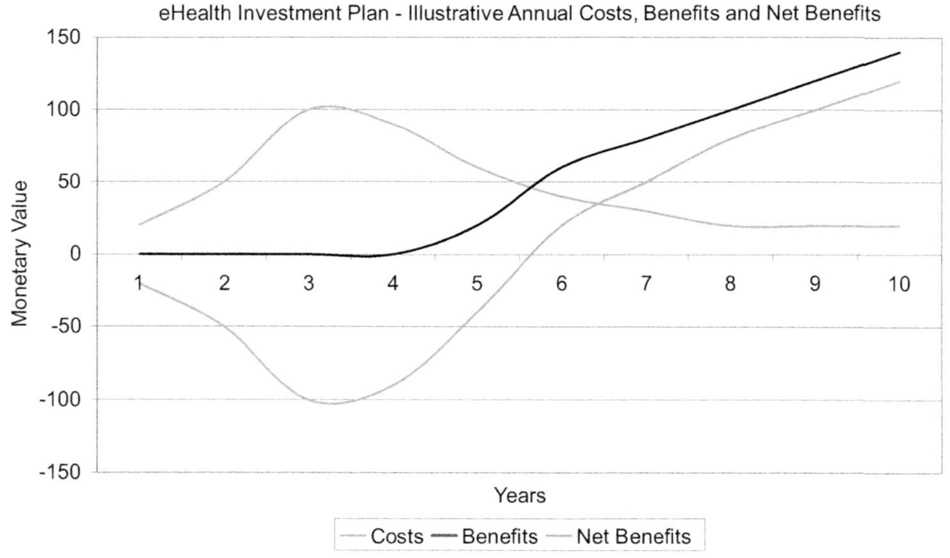

The eventual net benefit curve shows that the project offers value for money, justifying the investment of cash and other resources. The local nature of an e-health project determines the actual shape of the curves, but all e-health projects incur increased costs in the earlier years, with benefits realised after implementation, and with the objective of realising net benefits after that. An average time to realise net benefits is about four years (Stroetmann *et al.*, 2006). However, it can be more than ten years (EC, 2009a) for more complex projects such as EHRs. Reflecting this reality in the planned timescales of planned e-health projects helps to avoid increased risk, especially from unrealistic shortened timescales and so artificial, but disruptive cost and time overruns.

Not all e-health projects succeed. Chart 6 shows an outcome where benefits are insufficient to realise a net benefit over time; it shows a net socio-economic cost, not value for money, so the project does not justify the investment of cash and other resources. You can use your assessment to avoid this kind of situation.

Chart 6. Illustrative cost, benefit and net cost curves for an e-health project

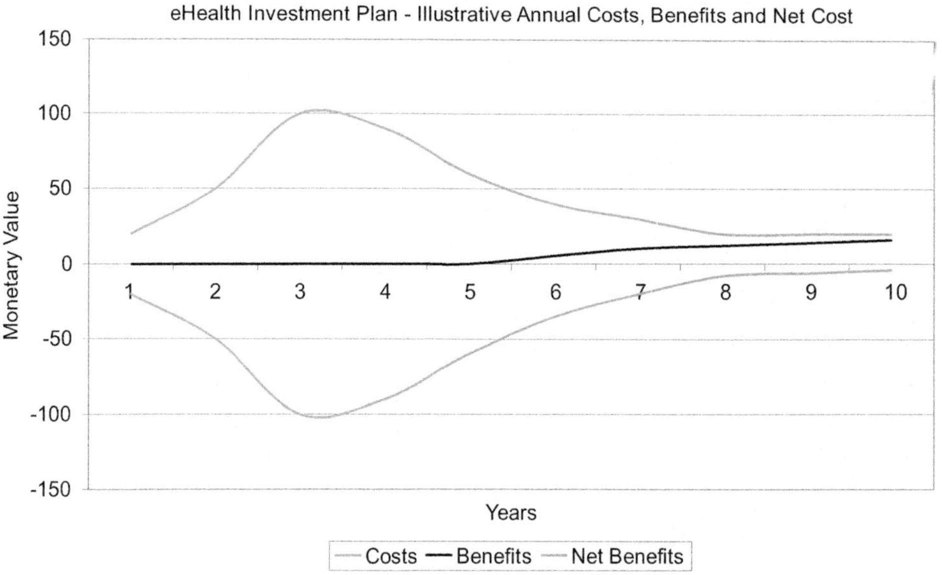

Where a project is heading in this direction, it needs either modifying significantly or stopping altogether to avoid drawing resources from projects that do offer value for money.

The whole e-health investment plan and programme is an aggregation of these types of curves. Embedded within these are the budgets and financing arrangements for each project. You will have to compile these separately in a spending plan that aggregates each project – see Table 17. You may want to copy this table into a spreadsheet.

Table 17. Illustrative budget and financing plan for an e-health project

E-health project A											
Years	*1*	*2*	*3*	*4*	*5*	*6*	*7*	*8*	*9*	*10*	*Total*
	$000	$000	$000	$000	$000	$000	$000	$000	$000	$000	$000
Resources											
Engagement											
Staff types redeployed, time and cost											
Extra staff types, time and cost											
Requirements											
Staff types redeployed, time and cost											
Extra staff types, time and cost											
Architecture											
Staff types redeployed, time and cost											
Extra staff types, time and cost											
Functionality											
Staff types redeployed, time and cost											
Extra staff types, time and cost											
Applications											
Staff types redeployed, time and cost											
Extra staff types, time and cost											
Usability											
Staff types redeployed, time and cost											
Extra staff types, time and cost											
Utilisation											
Staff types redeployed, time and cost											

E-health project A											
Years	*1*	*2*	*3*	*4*	*5*	*6*	*7*	*8*	*9*	*10*	*Total*
	$000	$000	$000	$000	$000	$000	$000	$000	$000	$000	$000
Extra staff types, time and cost											
Procurement											
Staff types redeployed, time and cost											
Extra staff types, time and cost											
Project Management											
Extra staff types, time and cost											
Training											
Staff types redeployed, time and cost											
Extra staff types, time and cost											
Change											
Staff types redeployed, time and cost											
Extra staff types, time and cost											
Benefits realisation											
Staff types redeployed, time and cost											
Extra staff types, time and cost											
ICT hardware, net cost											
ICT software, net cost											
ICT middleware, net cost											
ICT other net cost											
Others											
Staff types redeployed, time and cost											
Extra staff types, time and cost											

E-health project A

Years	*1*	*2*	*3*	*4*	*5*	*6*	*7*	*8*	*9*	*10*	*Total*
	$000	$000	$000	$000	$000	$000	$000	$000	$000	$000	$000
Skills and knowledge for the capacity action											
Staff types redeployed, time and cost											
Extra staff types, time and cost											
Financing											
Capital outlay											
Revenue outlay											
Capital finance											
Revenue finance											
Financing sources											
Differences											
Capital											
Revenue											
Risk adjusted											
Capital											
Revenue											
Risk exposures											
Risk mitigation measures											
Benefits											
Patients											
Healthcare professionals											
Healthcare organisations											
NGOs											

This information is essential to prepare proposals to release finance for each e-health project. A separate template is available for this called 'Proposals and Business Cases for E-Health Investment in Projects' (Commonwealth Secretariat, 2009b).

All e-health projects carry risks. It is essential that you identify, measure, manage and mitigate them. Your e-health investment plans must include realistic, robust arrangements for all activities that are to be included in the project management effort. Monitoring by the programme manager and appropriate executives must be explicit and frequent, with a requirement that they take appropriate decisions to minimise risks and preferably avoid them, although this is not always practical.

When you have completed you re-health investment and project plans, the next step is effective dissemination to the stakeholders. If you publish an e-health road map, it can help to inform citizens and health workers. This should use all available media, and include websites, radio, television, newspapers, community resource centres, 'train the trainer' teams and economic, social and political forums. A requirement for effective dissemination and communication through a wide range of media is to have a consistent content over time. The e-health investment plan is the source to achieve this.

CHAPTER 13

Benefits Realisation Plan

None of the previous effort is worthwhile unless benefits and net benefits are realised. This requires benefits realisation to be part of the e-health investment plan, and needs effort by users and organisations as part of each e-health project. Benefits are often realised from changes in clinical and working practices, leading to improvements in performance. It is essential that stakeholders are aware of the opportunities and challenges to improve health and healthcare through e-health, so they can contribute fully to realising benefits and amalgamate them with the range of other priorities for change.

There are two main types of benefit. One derives from the requirements of the health and healthcare strategy, the other is additional to them. For the benefits realisation plan, the strategic benefits and any significant high-value additional benefits need to be included. The aim is to move from the generic features such as quality, access and efficiency, and change models such as strategic, organic and process, to develop a set of measurable steps that lead to benefits realisation over a realistic timescale. To achieve this, it is important to identify the appropriate, significant dependencies of the e-health project components that have to be in specific sequences. Then, you need to link them together. The tasks involved are:

- Preparing an analysis of current service provision and performance before the start of the e-health programmes or projects, so that benefits realisation will be more achievable and measurable
- Developing supporting infrastructure
- Ensuring that stakeholders know the changes required and their role in realising these
- Setting up new clinical and working arrangements
- Removing or redeploying redundant resources.

These are complex tasks, and an effective way to approach them is to rely on teamwork between health and healthcare groups and to start benefits realisation at the outset of each e-health project. Benefits should be identified in the e-health investment plan described in chapter 12. Table 18 illustrates a schedule of activities for all e-health projects.

Table 18. Illustrative summary of benefits realisation activity and links

Benefit	*Dependency*	*Change*	*Leader*	*Start*	*Risks*
Project 1 More patient access	E-health 1 E-health 2	**Adopt:** Clinical practice 1 Clinical practice 2 Working practice 1 **Give up:** Working practice 21	Dr A	2010	Overrun Engagement Data security
Project 2 Fewer malaria cases	E-health 2 E-health 3	**Adopt:** Clinical practice 3 Clinical practice 4 Working practice 2 **Give up:** Working practice 22	Dr B	2011	Overrun Engagement Wrong e-health ICT infrastructure
Project 3 Lower child mortality	E-health 3 E-health 4	**Adopt:** Clinical practice 5 Clinical practice 6 Working practice 3 **Give up:** Working practice 23	Dr C	2012	Overrun Engagement Wrong e-health ICT infrastructure
Project 4 Fewer maternal deaths	E-health 3 E-health 5	**Adopt:** Clinical practice 3 Clinical practice 5 Working practice 4 **Give up:** Working practice 24	Dr D	2013	Overrun Engagement Wrong e-health ICT infrastructure

The separate supporting plan and table for benefits realisation needed for each e-health project will have detailed activities and practices. This should form part of each project plan and will be part of the whole e-health programme. It enables benefits realisation to maintain a driving role in project management. This is instead of the typical mad rush to spend the available money, achieving few future net benefits but sometimes a net cost, and often with high risk of failure.

Table 18 is a source of information for programme management. When your benefit realisation effort is underway, the progress updates the plan. If nothing happens, the routine review can trigger decisions and actions to deal with blockages and inhibitors, and this is valuable information for the programme board.

CHAPTER 14
Capacity

Capacity and capability are challenges for e-health investment in most countries. Indeed, these aspects set a greater challenge than the availability of finance for many EC countries (EC, 2009b). While capacity is a shared challenge, each country should set up its own measures to deal with it. At its simplest, the strategy is to employ more people with the required skills and knowledge. Success depends on a viable strategy, a plan, then action, as with the example below. When capacity needs enhancing for several parts of an e-health policy and strategy loop, what is already a complex issue becomes even more so.

Six areas for capacity development are leadership, ICT priorities, change, the e-health investment plan, implementation and benefits realisation. Developing e-health leadership as a first priority can often ensure that organisations are able to expand capacity in other areas.

Illustrative capacity strategy – there are several components. They should look forward about ten years and include strategies to:

- Develop e-health leaders who can engage and collaborate with stakeholders, especially healthcare professionals, and take and control effective e-health investment decisions through programme management
- Develop healthcare professionals to contribute to e-health investment, especially engagement and organisational change
- Develop rapid response technical support teams for all e-health initiatives
- Recruit, train, reward and retain people with health informatics skills and qualifications, and develop their skills in e-health
- Recruit, train, reward and retain people with programme and project management qualifications, and develop their skills in e-health
- Recruit, train, reward and retain people with ICT qualifications and skills such as ICT evaluation, implementation, operation and support, and develop their skills in e-health
- Recruit, train, reward and retain people with programme and project management qualifications, and develop their skills in e-health
- Recruit, train, reward and retain people with ICT procurement skills
- Invest in continuous awareness of ICT opportunities for health and healthcare
- Invest in e-learning as a resource to develop capacity.

Illustrative capacity plan – the components include to:

- Identify numbers of leaders and specialists needed for e-health over the next ten years
- Set up continuous e-health learning groups for executive and clinical leaders
- Work with ministries for technologies to set up ICT and e-health training facilities with local universities
- Set up a rapid response technical support team for current and planned e-health initiatives
- Work with ministries for technologies to set up programme and project management training facilities with local providers working within the principles of the Association of Project Managers[8]
- Create new reward packages for ICT and project managers to ensure their retention
- Set up a continuous database of ICT possibilities and opportunities for e-health, drawing from global initiatives and possibly shared with other countries
- Set up arrangements to train all the types of skills identified in the capacity strategy
- Set up e-learning facilities for e-health as part of life-long learning initiatives
- Sustain partnership working with healthcare professionals' organisations, other ministries, all types of healthcare provider organisations, ICT suppliers and education institutes and organisations.

Illustrative capacity action – the components include to:

- Convert plan into firm deliverables
- Implement financing and budget packages with appropriate stakeholders to support the capacity plan
- Agree training services from local universities, colleges and e-learning providers for skills such as programme and project management
- Recruit, train and retain people with the new skills identified in the capacity strategy, and assign them to projects as soon as they are available
- Assign the e-health workforce to a continuous e-health learning programme
- Integrate people with new e-health skills and knowledge into the workforce, especially working alongside doctors, nurses and other healthcare professionals.

Action should roll out to the points where citizens, patients and carers deal with health and healthcare activities, rather than from centralised initiatives. This should help to gain local ownership that can lead to sustainable capacity.

8. See: www.apm.org.uk [last accessed 3 August 2010].

CHAPTER 15

Evaluation, Implementation, Review and Feedback

Evaluation, implementation, review and feedback should provide the links between e-health performance and progress, short-term goals, medium-term plans and long-term strategies. These aspects match the e-health jigsaw model in the methodology and template and enable the stages of implementation and feedback, as shown in Chart 7.

Chart 7. Illustrative fit of health and healthcare strategies and plans with e-health strategies and plans

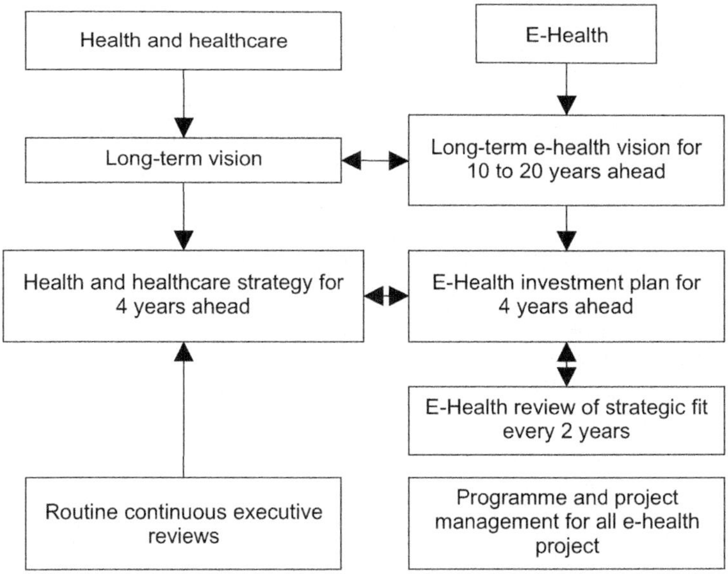

The essential themes are integrating the short-term e-health activity with the long-term e-health vision and health strategy. The new e-health opportunities that you create can provide new opportunities for the health and healthcare vision and strategy. A review of the short-term fit to health and healthcare strategies every two years is essential, because e-health is a high-value, high-risk investment, and the strategic fit needs managing well. Regular reviews on a short-term timescale help to sustain the strategic integration (Stroetmann *et al.*, 2006). This is especially important for e-health projects that rely on small-scale implementation and trials. Prompt evaluations can lead to decisions to scale-up e-health projects, avoid costly and wasteful project drift and to abandon failing projects promptly. This increases the emphasis on implementation and action. It also creates a knowledge base of e-health that succeeds and e-health that does not. This knowledge is essential to inform future e-health decisions.

As programme managers review progress, they can revise and update each section of the appropriate tables. Eventually, you will need a comprehensive review, probably after about two years, or earlier if major unexpected events have occurred. This feedback loop offers you a way to update your progress. From these, a reset e-health strategy will change costs, benefits and timescales for existing projects, and possibly abandon some completely. There may be a need to add new e-health priorities and projects to the e-health strategy, with a new e-health investment plan rolled forward.

The first stage of the review is to evaluate the impact that you have achieved. This could include a technical evaluation of the ICT and information standards, and a socio-economic evaluation of the relationship of all costs to all benefits over time. Both should reveal any changes needed. Achieving this relies on recognising that the e-health strategy and e-health investment plan are dynamic, changing documents. It is not essential to finalise every detail. Your plan can include evaluation and assessments scheduled for completion during the investment period, and so continue to inform e-health strategy and investment.

The aim is for you to identify the modest, affordable, practical steps to e-health development that can succeed within the available capacity. As this development moves ahead, it should create a cycle of increasing realism, success and investment in more e-health that advances the overall health and healthcare strategy. After each review, a new e-health road map can inform citizens and health workers.

When you use the workbook, please bear in mind that e-health is dynamic. Your tables are not a set of forms for completion all in one go. Policies, strategies and projects are always changing and developing, so your workbook is a way for you to decide how to drive it forward.

CHAPTER 16

Conclusion

Participants at the Commonwealth Secretariat's dialogues on e-health consistently highlighted their needs in preparing policies and strategies for e-health in their countries. The Commonwealth Secretariat welcomed their proposal to prepare a generic workbook for widespread use.

You can use the workbook in many different ways. You can use it to help you to make decisions for your e-health strategy and to identify the policy issues that you need to address. It is best to use it in workshops with a team of people from many different backgrounds, such as senior civil servants responsible for health, healthcare, ICT and finance; doctors; nurses; healthcare managers; ICT managers; and ICT suppliers. A team like this often has different views and ideas and using the workbook can help to put these together.

You can use this workbook to as a checklist for the agenda and topics for the team. You can use the parts that are most important to you and you can change and add to the templates so they fit your precise needs better. The templates are designed for users to modify easily and are available in Microsoft Word from the Secretariat's website http://www.thecommonwealth.org/ehealth

Rarely are e-health policies and strategies completed once for a five to ten year period. New techniques and technologies emerge rapidly and sometimes unexpectedly; for example, some telemedicine initiatives are feasible as part of m-health projects, so would probably not be part of an e-health strategy written five years ago.

The e-health dialogues revealed two important matters relevant to the way that you use the workbook. One is that countries are at very different positions and stages of e-health development, so they will begin from different places as they construct their e-health policies and strategies. Second, there are many people in each country with considerable skills and expertise in a wide range of e-health activities. They provide the essential sources of leadership and knowledge, and this workbook will help them to marshal and review their ideas, decisions and priorities in collaboration with their colleagues. These skilled teams are the source of your e-health policies and strategies.

References

Africa Health Infoway: http://www.who.int/africahealthinfoway/en/index.html [last accessed 20 July 2010].

Amarasingham, R, L Plantinga, M Diener-West, D J Gaskin and N R Powe (2009) *Clinical Information Technologies and Inpatient Outcomes: A Multiple Hospital Study*. Archives of Internal Medicine, 169(2) pp.108–114. Available at: http://archinte.ama-assn.org/cgi/content/full/169/2/108 [last accessed 20 July 2010].

Commission of the European Communities (CEC) (2004) *e-Health – making healthcare better for European citizens: An action plan for a European e-Health Area*, Communication from the Commission to the Council, the European Parliament, the European Economic and Social Committee and the Committee of the Regions. Available at: http://ec.europa.eu/information_society/doc/qualif/health/COM_2004_0356_F_EN_ACTE.pdf [last accessed 17 July 2010].

Commonwealth Secretariat (2009a) *e-health Capacity Assessment – e-health Situation Analysis Questionnaire*. London: Commonwealth Secretariat. Available at: http://www.thecommonwealth.org/ehealth

Commonwealth Secretariat (2009b) Proposals and Business Case Templates for e-health Projects in Commonwealth Countries 20 April 2009. London: Commonwealth Secretariat. Available at: http://www.thecommonwealth.org/ehealth

Dobrev, A, T Jones, V N Stroetmann, K A Stroetmann, Y Vatter and K Peng (2009) *The socio-economic impact of interoperable electronic health record (EHR) and ePrescribing systems in Europe and beyond*. European Commission. Available at: http://www.ehr-impact.eu/downloads/documents/EHRI_final_report_2009.pdf [last accessed 20 July 2010].

EC (2007) eHealth Impact Project, Directorate General Information Society and Media. Brussels: EC. Available at: http://www.ehealth-impact.org/ [last accessed 17 July 2010].

EC (2009a) Electronic Health Record and ePrescribing Project. Brussels: Directorate General Information Society and Media, EC. Available at: www.ehr-impact.eu [last accessed 17 July 2010].

EC (2009b) Boosting E-Health Investment, Directorate General Information Society and Media. Brussels: EC. Available at: www.financing-ehealth.eu [last accessed 17 July 2010].

European Commission Information Society and Media Directorate-General (EC ISMDG) (2007) Accelerating the Development of the eHealth Market in Europe, eHealth Task Force Report.

Goldsbrough, D, E Adovor and B Eldberger (2007) *What has happened to health spending and fiscal flexibility in low-income countries with IMF programs?* Working Group on IMF Programs and Health Expenditures, Center for Global Development, April 2007.

Jones, T, A Dobrev, K Stroetmann, V Stroetmann, P Wilson and P Drury (2008) *E-Health for Developing Countries: Affordable Strategies*. London: Commonwealth Secretariat. Available at: http://www.thecommonwealth.org/files/177214/FileName/HMM_G__08_3-EHealthforDevelopingCountries_2_.pdf [last accessed 21 July 2010].

Kamunyo, P (undated) Quality Care and Cost Containment Making Private Health Insurance More Affordable, AKI Presentation.

Otieno, G (2006) Nokia Mobile Authentication Solution, presentation 19 December 2006.

The Rockefeller Foundation (RF) (2008) Bellagio E-Health Call to Action. Available at: http://www.ehealth-connection.org/content/bellagio-ehealth-call-action [last accessed 17 July 2010].

Scott, N, S Batchelor, J Ridley and B Jorgensen (2004) *The Impact of Mobile Phones in Africa*. Commission for Africa, November 2004.

Stroetmann, KA, T Jones, A Dobrev and V N Stroetmann (2006) *eHealth is Worth it: The economic benefits of implemented eHealth solutions at ten European sites*. European Commission Information Society and Media Directorate General. Available at: http://www.ehealthimpact.org/download/documents/ehealthimpactsept2006.pdf [last accessed 20 July 2010].

United Nations Foundation/Vodafone Foundation (UNF/VF) (undated) *mHealth for Development: The Opportunity of Mobile Technology for Healthcare in the Developing World*, Factsheet. Available from: http://www.globalproblems-globalsolutions-files.org/unf_website/assets/publications/technology/mhealth/mHealth_for_Development_Report_1Pager.pdf [last accessed 20 July 2010].

WHO (2005) *Connecting for Health: Global Vision, Local Insight*, Report on the World Summit for the Information Society, ISBN 92 4 159390 3. Available at: http://www.who.int/kms/resources/WSISReport_Connecting_for_Health.pdf [last accessed 17 July 2010].

WHO (2006a) *Electronic Health Records: A Manual for Developing Countries*, ISBN 92 9061 2177. Available at: http://www.wpro.who.int/NR/rdonlyres/5753F8CF-8A78-4639-BEFC-F0EE-9B3CBA0A/0/EHRmanual.pdf [last accessed 17 July 2010].

WHO (2006b) *eHealth Tools and Services: Needs of the Member States*, Report of the WHO Global Observatory for E-Health. Available at: http://www.who.int/kms/initiatives/tools_and_services_final.pdf [last accessed 17 July 2010].

WHO (2006c) *Building foundations for eHealth*, Report of the WHO Global Observatory for E-Health, ISBN 978 92 4 159504 9. Available at: http://www.who.int/goe/publications/

WHO (2007) *Everybody's Business: Strengthening Health Systems to Improve Health Outcomes*, WHO's Framework for Action, ISBN 978 92 4 159607 7. Available at: http://www.wpro.who.int/NR/rdonlyres/5BA80B95-DC1F-4427-8E8B-0D9B1E9AF776/0/EB.pdf [last accessed 17 July 2010].

Yunkap Kwankam, S and RJ Richardson (2007) 'Improving health in the Commonwealth: the role and importance of e-health as an enabling environment', *Commonwealth Health Ministers Reference Book 2007*. London: Henley Media Group for the Commonwealth Secretariat.

Printed in Dunstable, United Kingdom

91338346R00045